HOWE·LIBRARY

HANOVER
NEW HAMPSHIRE

WHAT TO TIP THE BOATMAN?

WHAT TO TIP THE BOATMAN?

Cleopatra Mathis

THE SHEEP MEADOW PRESS

RIVERDALE-ON-HUDSON, NEW YORK

All inquiries and permission requests should be addressed to:
The Sheep Meadow Press, Post Office Box 1345,
Riverdale-on-Hudson, New York 10471.

Designed and typeset by S.M.

COVER: J. M. W. Turner, *Slavers Throwing Overboard The Dead and
Dying—Typhon Coming On* (Museum of Fine Arts, Boston)

Photo of Cleopatra Mathis: Ted Rosenberg

This publication is made possible with public funds from the New
York State Council on the Arts, a state agency.

Library of Congress Cataloging-in-Publication Data:

Mathis, Cleopatra, 1947-
    What to tip the boatman? / Cleopatra Mathis
        p. cm.
    ISBN 1-878818-91-0 (acid-free paper) / 1-878818-97-X (pbk.)
        1. Mother and child—Poetry. 2. Motherhood—Poetry.
    3. Mothers—Poetry. I. Title.

PS3562.A8363 W48 2001
811'.54--dc21

                                            00-053144

For Simon, Tessa, Alexandra, and Zachary

—and for Deborah Knapp (1979-1993)

ACKNOWLEDGEMENTS

Grateful acknowledgment is made to the following magazines and journals where these poems, or versions of them, first appeared.

The Georgia Review: "The Betrayal"
Louisiana Literature: "What disappears"
Ploughshares: "Fall at Wellfleet Beach," "Saving Herself," "What to Tip the Boatman?"
Poetry: "Demeter the Pilgrim," "Living Here"
River City: "Two Girls"
Seneca Review: "Solstice"
Smartish Pace: "Persephone, Answering," "The Ruin," "Reconciled"
The Southern Review: "The Bow," "Figure of Formal Loss: Pearl," "Fist," "History" (published as "Life of Elvis"), "The Goodbye," "Something to Save"
Tri-Quarterly: "as if mad is a direction, like west," "After Persephone," "Old Trick," "White Primer"
The Yale Review: "Demeter"
Washington Square: "6 A.M.," "Presentiment"

"Under Moose Mountain," "Noon," "Search," and "The Return" first appeared in *The Breath of Parted Lips*: *Voices from the Robert Frost Place,* CavanKerry Press, Ft. Lee, N.J.

"That Year" first appeared in the anthology *Under the Legislature of Stars,* Oyster River Press, Lee, N.H.

I am grateful to the Corporation of Yaddo, The MacDowell Colony, and Dartmouth College for fellowships during the writing of this book. My deepest thanks to Pamela Harrison for her invaluable reading of these poems as they moved through various stages.

"as if mad is a direction, like west . . ." is taken from the novel *Alias Grace* by Margaret Atwood; the poem is for Ariana Funaro.

"Ocular Occlusion" is for John Skoyles.

CONTENTS

I.

II.

"Against Persephone's will Hades took her by the design of Zeus
with his immortal horses . . .
He snatched the unwilling maid into his golden chariot
and led her off lamenting . . .

The mountain peaks and the depths of the sea echoed
in response to her divine voice, and her goddess mother heard.
Sharp grief seized her heart, and she tore the veil
on her ambrosial hair with her own hands.
She cast a dark cloak on her shoulders
and sped like a bird over dry land and sea,
searching. No one was willing to tell her the truth,
not one of the gods or mortals . . .
For mortals she ordained a terrible and brutal year
on the deeply fertile earth. The ground released
no seed, for bright-crowned Demeter kept it buried."

—from the *Homeric Hymn to Demeter*
trans. Helene Foley

I.

THE OWL

How far did she fly to find
this pristine town on the edge of winter?
Crows have set up their kingdom—
a yacking flock louder than traffic
maims the morning air.
Day sends the coven screaming
in pursuit, black rags
haggling from clump to clump

of the decorous elms and oaks.
The dog's mouth hangs.
I follow his gaze through the shudder
of limbs to the still source, the center
of their flapping. The barn owl
commands a branch, the crows scatter
and aim, cutting around her
placid weight, something more of earth

than air. She stares straight ahead
as if focused on something she alone
can hear, their outrage at who she is
no more than a furious snipping,
until in one motion, she heaves upward,
her body transformed by sky.
The crows gloat, their battering
closes her path, and she misses a beat,
stumbling in the air
like a silence disrupted. The crows'
fat riot, their *mine, mine, mine,*
rules the sky. Call the owl
sadness, the one who watches
from the other side.

OLD TRICK

Spring wants me back,
and I should know better than to heed
that old hag, the goddess
disguising herself with the first green
she can muster. Her true self hanging around,
gray, icy, bent, gazing from the corners
while I glory in the fine scribble
skimming the trees. I let her
bear the weight of my heart,
not my first mistake: every year she promises

to bring back what I love, and for awhile
she does—a flower here, another there,
fast-talking me through the price
I'll pay later. It's one panorama
followed by the next, the returning
birds in a parade, finches
twittering at dawn. They too

make you think you can trust them:
look at those nests, their faith
at your feeder, but I can tell you this,
keep an eye on the children.
September will come, the ripe business
whirring—everything
you can't see in all the greenery,
its constancy already tinged: a slight cast,
a whine. Your own girl will vanish
under that yellowing wing.

SOLSTICE

1.

The child, thirteen, pushing away
the clip that tamed her hair.
The child with a pistol against her ear.
In the great life of things, a small noise
against the noise of spring. So small,
the mother downstairs only heard
the sound of something falling.

2.

She went, young enough to believe
nothingness is an empty field—
so many blackbirds out there you couldn't see,
wings with their red and yellow bars, the one
clear note coming from somewhere, a nest
to settle in. Where she fell, a world
would rise to hold her.
Isn't that what the story teaches?

3.

They stumble in the yard, the parents
leading all the classmates
stunned around them. Just beyond the funeral
heat, a meadow burns in the glare,
the new hay pales.
Every parent invents a story.

4.

No one knew she wanted the dark, that girl
whispering into a book—
already a woman's tongue, an eye.
A last shake of her hair, and another world
took her words, the ground opened
for her bones. She's under the nursery-grown
tree's accomplished shape, a small fact fixed
between the pine and lilac.
She was young enough to want a home down there
And the ghost you've heard for months now,
that's what failure sounds like:
explaining and explaining.

NOON

1.

What adolescent can bear her mother?
Her words, her touch. The baby
who hung to my ample thigh
veers away, whips her horse
to go faster. She's testing
this gelding; she'll have him
charging through the afternoon—her reckless will
aiming for that surge
in the chest, the swallow of romantic dark.

2.

Something's wrong. The day's brilliance
shakes the horse. His eyes whiten,
he throws his head—some command
bears down from the heaven
of sun-eaten blue. Circling, circling,
the girl uses what she knows:
leg grip, seat, the danger
of showing the horse her fear
I can't stop him, her voice level
as they bolt past. The field's sod rips
and heaves, black ruts
open for the stumble.

All I can think is how calm she is,
caught in a race that promises
to send her flying. Now she's forward
in the saddle, willing to go

with what's been given.
Flushed, steady, her hands
hold quiet, cupping the reins
as she's been taught.

TWO GIRLS

They play a kind of house, with animals
instead of dolls. The cats rounded up,
the one grouchy dog. When reluctance
stiffens the cats to a low-pitched whine,
the dog tearing at his little skirt,
they make horses of each other,
each with her reins of hair, the braids
they take turns trotting behind, whinnying,
breaking into a canter around the yard.
By eleven, they're saving mustangs, two girls
with their posters in the pet food aisle
to fight against horse flesh in Alpo.

What happens then? What midnight
persuades them to leave the house
that first time on the deserted road?
We're asleep in our beds. We don't know
about the Tarot, the dealt cards
turning up the swords: three in a heart,
eight over a hidden face, nine
surrounding the girl, blind and bound.
They take the ferryman with the two huddled figures
to the Ouija board, where they go back and forth
with the dead. We don't hear them
down at our own river—talk about the half-sunk
boat left on the inlet, how they plan
to fix it, go somewhere, anywhere.
We think we know what lives inside those heads.

GRADUATION PARTY

The last time we saw her, she clowned
for all the kids, sacrilege
in her every refusal: eighth grade
she seemed to know was a joke,
mean and trite. Every typical gesture
brought her wry remark. The boys, of course,
loved her scorn far more
than prettiness, pushing her into the pool,
her shriek as close as they could get.
Tired of fancy dives, one boy
in a last reach to win approval
threw his goggles hard. An edge of plastic
caught her just above the eye.
Consternation and the blood
called me out—hovering, anxious
that her mother would whisk the child away,
breaking the life of the party.

I led the girl inside and washed her face,
calculated the damage, relieved.
No need for stitches, for any solace
but a bandaid. And she had already
shrugged off the incident, indifferent
to any pain, planning even then
to leave us all.

THAT YEAR

Winter nailed itself to the ground.
My girl was fourteen, breaking and freezing.
She'd slice another hole in her body,
not pierces but a ragged stitch
circling her arm.
March came, the bad snow
kibbled to rot. Dog-kicked, hungry days
ate at her; a red slash
streaked through her chopped hair.
More in bed than not,
she wanted her black room, the walls lined
with pictures: Cobain sprawled
dead in his Converse All-Stars, rabbits
tortured for eye make-up, the clubbed seal's fur.
Everywhere she looked: the unyielding world.
She rubbed her own cut fingers into the evidence
hanging there, the perfect smiles, anorexic
and bulimic, the baby in the toilet, the stalker.

Outside, I turned my back
to the prevailing weather, studied
my good preparations—gardens I'd planted
in last fall's rain. The weeks would come
in the order of snowdrops, crocuses,
daffodils, tulips. I'd planted according
to every specification, the good mother
charting soil and depth and food.
Everything in my rich dirt was sure to rise.

PRESENTIMENT

Tides, current, wind—
I'm as unfaithful as they are.
So full of noise I never heard
her crying. I didn't see
her changing face—too busy
riding the wave of my obligation.
I've got a job, the world
calls me. How many times
did I tell her this?

I took her everywhere. She's there
in all the pictures. The group of artists
arranged according to our gifts,
word or deed. I'm the only one
cradling a child. Asked, I would have said
my work suffered. I envied the others
giving into whim, like children themselves.
Working when they pleased, all night
at bars, the one dance joint.
Off-season in that seaside town,

chattering, she tagged along.
I was trying to say something
about pastures: the endless ocean
bringing forth those crenellated lives
like so many spiked grasses . . .
I let her climb the sea wall,
a balancing act in those baby steps
tottering above the crash of the tide.
Even the fisherman hauling his net
motioned to catch my eye.

A mother can't look away.
The day bloomed, caught her
while I gloried, wild with praise
for my own weather. For a few seconds
the water buoyed her body up,
a small flag on the surface.

THE REFUSAL

When she heard her daughter fall,
the mother's world closed
in one shot, a history divided.
Across the river, I went on
with my life, not noticing
my own child push past me
to the bus stop, black jacket, black skirt.
And later, every inch covered,
her face averted so I wouldn't ask
about the straight-edge razor
or cigarette lighter in her room. I didn't see
how she could harm her body—a mother's prized
landscape of lily and rose, neck, cheek . . .
A destruction so gradual, at first
I called it accidental, believing her shrug
about the bruise from nowhere, the apple knife
slipping, or the story about a boy who shoved
a burning wad of paper in her blouse.

A natural order gone wrong, the dismantling
of some glorious thing—who could understand,
in the trees' bounty of perfected greens,
the logic of one leaf
withering, then another, limb to limb—
until one morning, I couldn't recognize the girl at all.
Realization came like the circle of a lie,
the one that promised plenitude,
leading me back to ignorance, my genius
for self-deceit. And I keep calling,
naming every power: man, woman, God;
offering every gift, down to my prideful body,

begging to get her back.
But no—the day turns
its black cloak, a gaping hole.

FOR MONTHS

I dragged out of my hard sleep,
dense with its journeys,
dreading the moment which returned me
to the stairs leading to her room.
I couldn't move, fearing
each step toward the evidence
of blades I kept taking away:
warned first by the walls,
not their writhing forms, but colors
tipped with a drying red that told me
she'd found some new place on her body to hate.
I'd travel through her rage
to find her flung on the bed—lucky arrival
if all I saw were old signs
of cuts and bruises.

I'd wait. I had so far to go
in absolute stillness, dying
to hear some small sound of her breath,
an inhalation, a turn, her life
just resting. The hell of the place
had wormed itself inside me so deep
I couldn't climb out. The little self
closed up tight, refusing to speak
unless she woke—the bargain
that replaced every other.

THE TUNNEL

After the shrink with his overstuffed chair,
after the scream that sliced
the pastel air, after all the parents
took their turns with pleas and bribes,
long after the rain at the window turned to sleet
and night fell—the girl slipped
into the tunnel she had dug barehanded,
turning on us one last time
her stranger's eye. Through our panic
to find a lock to keep her,
a hospital to hold her,
she had one word left
and she shot it at us, venom to the ones
who tried to bar her way. One word
to shepherd her through the holding ward
to the basement maze of burrowing labs
where they drew the legitimate blood,
one polite tube; one word to court and marry
as they wheeled her along the turning
passage of concrete halls, one word
echoing *dead, dead, dead.*

WHITE PRIMER

Even the clock is a liar:
the clouds' blank ceiling
claims whatever light falls from the sky.
I wake to the day, an arrow
aiming for the hour to call the nurse,
caretaker of the new white world
where my daughter lives, all her color
stripped in the name of health.
Doesn't the snow come to let the earth live?
So too will they cover the girl with white,
all that raging blossom of the self.

Don't ask me to believe in this season.
White nametag, white gown, the red lesions
like roads going nowhere. Covered, you see,
by the weather of this place:
you will not, you will not, you will not

until she hears it like a heartbeat in the white tempest.
All passion spent, all will,
she is good enough for the allowed visit,
the allowed room. Led to her,
I can't read the map of her cold face.
Nothing reveals the child I know
but the hopeless tangle of her hair.

SEARCH

An itch I couldn't get to
lived in my eyes. I scratched,
they burned. No make-up, no balm,
I clutched the wheel, I drove
through the rural wash of snow and salt
to the hospital. The enemy's address

was somewhere in her head. I drove
in and out of blackness, smelled the shit
on the farmers' road. My eyes swelled to slits,
narrowed, hardened. Yes, I'd be a bird of prey,
I'd go after the dark.
                              Led to her,
I took her face in my hands, peered
as if to find the small child she'd been,
the infant, the embryo. I wanted her
so far back she'd disappear inside me.

I couldn't find the way in. I couldn't see
into her face, which had become like clay
shaped by pills and needles into no look at all.
Nothing but the inward
listening to the god of the backwards clock.

CUTLERY

You must earn the fork,
but only after you've earned
the spoon. All you'll know
of the knife
is the blade you remember,
cousin to the fork's five prongs,
those scissored lines
you dragged along your arm.
Points for the healing,
points to earn anything
hell-bent for damage.
Nothing's innocent, not
in this world. You'll eat
like the civilized only before
dismissal through the double
metal door. Ignore that bell
from the other side: the visitor
you'll have to earn as well.
You're the zero
on heaven's chart.
Nothing's for you
but this plate of white food.
Two fingertips and one thumb
will make a clever tool.
Hungry enough, you'll slave
to institutional hours.
It's twelve: you eat,
at one you'll speak.

Don't want to eat?
Don't want to speak?
We'll have to put you all alone

in the metal bed in the metal room
with all the metal lights
turned out. Pound,
and stirrups will hold you down.
Scream, and it's double
time, twice the fear
that makes you open up the scabs
in the Solitary Room, where you hear
the little voice of the one
that brought you,
the one that won't quit
breathing in your ear.

"as if mad is a direction, like west . . . "

I'm caught in March, the humdrum
ice-snow-ice fusing to a single gray.
I live on the road, headache

reeling to backache, hospital
to home, nowhere hours, hinged
and strung to her string of hours

in an unmapped hell. Where's the lock,
thread to the ultimate
pattern-maker, puppet-master

of the wires that make her jump?
I navigate the rut, my numb feet
dance—on the brake, on the gas—

leaping the back-road curves. I'm
programmed in a moving blur,
mother emblem, a stick-figure

doll to the daughter who jerks
and cries. Bent behind the fixed wheel,
I'm a blond smile in a black car,

unstitched. She's got the needle.

THE RUIN

When I was young, it was enough
to save myself. Childhood's house gave way
to the birds of the night, the rich
Louisiana dark which in its green
carries melody and chorus.
I set my own clock to it, rising
to rain in leaves, a voice
that told me I could leave that place.
Even later, the sun reflecting the image
of water onto a bedroom ceiling
could wake me.

But when my daughter disappeared,
no beauty gave back a reason to live.
I was nothing but mother, I would blow out
the world's candle. No burning,
no fire with its regeneration,
not even ash, that little cold ruin.
It was then I understood
the nothingness of the sea,
the crush of waves driven across miles,
riptides and currents deepening
in a water too vast to freeze.
Thousands of feet, impenetrable:
no diver, no machine, could breathe
in the time it took to reach that bottom;
nothing could live in that black, the descending
zones that cancelled out creatures—
the tiniest slime of protoplasm, eggy scum
on the chalky mud, whatever design
managed to quiver 300 fathoms down
to the zero of the final zone.

And everything above rendered trivial
by the great salt body rocking
through the sea floor canyons and mountains.
All of it a locked tomb, and me
in my iron boat.

LITTLE MAP

1.

All through her babyhood
I made her sickness mine,
breathing in her hot breath,
fever pushing
the thermometer's red vein.
One long night, I saved her,
climbed with her
into the shock of the cold bath.
On her year-old face, stillness
reigned, more terrifying

than when she screamed. By three
she'd found her own dark way
down the hallway to the toilet.
Divorce, daycare, the list
of sitters. What was that name
she yelled in her sleep; where was I
driving, running; where, on what road?
I sent her to bed, I let her cry.
I said no. I let her climb

to the topmost slide in the park
of rides. All children under six must be
accompanied, the plain sign read.
Afraid of heights, I watched her,
step by step, unwavering, until she turned
and laid the white sheepskin down,
while the wind pulled her braids out straight
and rattled the old tin slide. In the high air,
precise, she gave a push
and plummeted down.

2.

Anger, bitterness, grief:
a door slammed closed
in her old pink room. Every spirit
has its map. Watching her sleep,
I sit for hours, propped against her wall,
searching for clues in a new *I Spy*,
as if the danger lay in objects.
But whatever she has hidden
is in her head: I can't find the way
to lead this craziness home.

Slice my arm with a paperclip?
Dig roads to veins in the elbow's bend?
Who could follow
through that wilderness.
The last time we found
a small clearing, we sat with her,
doctor and concerned family
in our circling chairs—where terrified,
we watched her take her wrist apart
with nothing but one finger's nail.

SELF-PORTRAIT WITH HORSE

Her room emptied of everything
but light, her healing body
a canvas, she's drawn herself
as a scribble of hair, black gnarl
on the paper's white sheet.
Then an outline of the cracked
animal she tamed with her own hand
and the lines that hold him to her
in this forest of ends.
She's stripped to the essential, the saved
tangle of hair
wild around the face she made
into a heart, wall-eyed,
still beating.

INTERMEDIARY

When she came back, my daughter
brought November's moonless nights,
hunters and frenzied deer,
gunfire over the hill—a world
exposed under the bare trees.
She heard the dogs, and didn't sleep.
And though I couldn't stay awake,
I wouldn't leave her room,
tea at my elbow, my arms crossed
to prop me up. Vigilance was all I had,
unlike the hospital, the ones who taught her
to use what she knew, a medicine
in small doses; how to go back
and forth, traversing darkness
as if it were a footpath. It was hell to me,
watching from the other side
of the one-way glass. All I could hear
was the slight buzz of fluorescence,
the stainless walls guarding
her white skin. I couldn't touch
for fear of leaving some mark; my hands
might hold her back from the work
she had to do. They'd hardly let me visit.

I was no guardian. I never knew
what she knew, never followed
through the woods, down to the river,
the abandoned tracks running beside it,
useless steel in the litter and weeds.
Her new habits frightened me, her mouth
a stranger's, a tic in the pause
before she let herself speak, the healed

crosswork of cuts under the chiseled
blue stone that hung at her neck.
She'd found another mother, a faith
that pulled her from bed,
guided her across the swollen river
posted with warnings, where the trucks
loaded up the carcasses.
Cigarettes flickered, an oil fire
blazed in a drum, sign of the season,
and she waited there,
a knitted skull cap pulled low;
waited for the men, asking
How will you bless this?
How far can you carry this meat?

THE HORSE

In those days, she woke only
to reach the stable, the saddle.
Broken racehorse, tethered to his own hell,
he was the only one she'd ride.
She had him tamed on the lunge line
in the indoor ring, where he trusted
the calm circle around her, fixed on course.
That frozen afternoon, who knows what crack
he heard when she dropped the line?
Maybe her body scrambling to retrieve it
jogged his stubborn terror and turned him
crashing through the corridor of closed doors,
splintering each gate, the attached line
flying like a whip at his head, all the way
into the snow, where she followed
his twisting bloody trail. Three icy hours
the mercury dropped, the vet sewed,
steam rising from open flesh, the gaping
shoulder and neck, while in the horse's ear
she whispered him back—mother then
to his misery, rescued and changed.

6 A.M.

What turns the world?
The woods shift in the light
slicing the layered haze.
Veils and mirrors, green-sheeted,
move around the moment
where I stand, head tilted,
as if to hear my girl
sleeping somewhere on this hill.
A tense silence
spins at some mute center.
Left to nothing but my voice, I call,
giving my whole body to the sound,
claiming the four heavy syllables of her name.

The only answer is the wing
of wind, a wildness
veering through the treetops,
bending the birches.
Calling into that noise
is like calling into the sea.
Once in another dawn I stood
on the edge of rage, sea and sky
under one black hood,
holding a starfish, the children's trophy.
Knowing the pail of water wouldn't keep
through the long drive home,
I'd brought it down before they woke.
I threw the creature
hard into the storm, saw its arms
clutching in the rain's weight.
Sensate thing, I thought, troubled
I had not simply laid it down

at the water's mouth. Even then,
it seemed an omen. My voice rose,
the wind sent back its howl.

What could I
have been asking for? I'm a speck
in this vastness, the spent green
of the August field I wade through,
crying into the earthbound trees,
clumsy tongue in a faulty language
summoned from my body, reaching for hers.
The girl has another defender,
consort, a god she believes
will not refuse her.
Curtained in the woods, she burrows
deeper into her cover, willing
her body blind to shut me out.

DEI GRATIA

Lent again. I claim silence
against the long black day. The girl
with the burden folded on her back
lets the screen door slam as she hikes
into the gray-white of March.

One year since the hospital,
since the work of winter
held her in its vise, and I'm asked
to let her go, as if
what she carries now can save her.
In the finest sleet, she says
she'll make a fire, watching with her dog
the lucent veil flying
afternoon into night. The wind-torn

pines, hooded moon—under these,
Christ, what is my faith,
when even blessed Peter said *no*
and *no* and *no*? Even he would fail
because he was afraid.

Unable to summon the light of his transformation,
I cannot understand
how she lies there, the little heat of her breath
condensing to ice on the surface
of the deep layers, listening
all the unforgiven night.

ART PRESENTATION, SENIOR YEAR

She's made a box and put the dead friend in it:
a picture of a girl, thirteen, still smiling.
Not yet the girl with a gun, a pistol
pointed at her right ear. Nothing shows
but gold, her earring, a gleaming
at the heart of my own girl's work.

Here's the world of little things:
belongings from their eighth-grade year
laid in a box, point of departure
for two girls, one now
sealed with paint and clay by the other
who lived among the dead

to blame us all. She lights a candle
to put in the box, aspects of blue
drawn thick with vines.
But the gold light inside
turns the ivy to veins, a body
driven by the sun that blooms inside—

illuminating a window we look through
to see a girl resting. And I see then
the map, the lifeline of the daughter
who found her way back to be our guide.
The anger sleeps in the shape of a child
who will stay always a child—left there

by the young woman before us, her calm hands
moving to lay the girl down.

AFTER PERSEPHONE

Heaven got sweeter, its paperweight curve
star-crazy at its purple center.
She'd found a god, a weapon in the works.
Something I hadn't noticed in the field
fought out of the layers and took her.
I tore away the land's every color,
withered the smallest grasses. Every heartbeat
went blank, I dismantled the ticking.

They only say what I took, not what I gave:
roots and strong light, glory
in the single shoot, green currency
of the just-born. From the irredeemable,
the buried—this is how a self gets made.
Remember, that darkness contained the seed
sealed in the swollen red globe.
Hell had to pay.

THE RETURN

You magic thing, you brother,
erupting from underneath,
swallowing up whatever you wish.
Not enough to own everything below
this ground I govern—no,
you with your kingdom of rocks
took my one uncut jewel.
Something new to turn this way and that
on your throne down there.
Now she's eaten the earth's seeds,
you have to give her up. She'll be back,
but never with that innocence
you wanted.

We'll both have her, but it's nothing
more than a bargain she's bound to keep.
She's carved a self now—not for you or me.
Look how carefully,
gleaming in the light,
she rows herself out.

MAKING A LIFE

When the goddess spoke, she said
we'd have to make a world
inside this one—the flawed and damaged one
we received out of her pain.
Standing under the spring trees,
even now I want to believe in their innocence,
pastels and fringework of greens,
but what in the history of this earth
teaches anything but submission?

To make something shapely of a life!
Think of the smell of a newborn's hair,
the silk breast against the sheet, the nap
in the way the grass grows, resisting my heel.
In the moment's shine, the self
preserves the self, insistent

in memory. As vivid as any sickness
I recall the children's voices
moving through the wild thicket, their bodies
clumsy as small bears against the canes.
Brambles fought their shirts, one tug
setting off a minor earthquake, blackberries falling
in the bushes' wake. The children licked
their pricked fingers; the dark juices
marked their mouths. In that Eden

they enter and re-enter with their reedy tones,
my voice answering—that mother language
weaving and knotting this tapestry.
Summer buzzed and rose, the cloud of August
descending. They don't all come from Hades,
do they, those tiny winged creatures of the air?

II.

SOMETHING TO SAVE

Circling, the leaves above me
find the ground, by now invisible,
and I lie down in them
thinking of babies. In all
my running days, I thought I'd find one.
Not in the vine-filled ditch
thick with yellow buds each spring,
but lost in leaves,
a little body almost covered over.
I have my girl, my boy, two others
like my own, the nephew and niece
I'd take in a blink. Why this
longing for the found one,
the still live, pale child
from nowhere, her face closed
to whatever she's seen?
I'd tuck her inside my shirt,
rushing for warmth
on this day when the wind will
finish with the leaves,
nothing so final as their gold
wasted on the ground.

WHAT TO TIP THE BOATMAN?

Delicate—the way at three she touched
her hands tip to tip, each finger a rib
framing the tepee of her hands.
So tentative that joining, taking
tender hold of her body, as if the ballast
of her selfhood rested there. Already
she could thread tiny beads through the eye
and onto string, correctly placing
each letter of her name, sorting
thin black lines to make an alphabet,
the needle just so in her little hand.
She loved that necklace less
than cat's cradle, a game to weave
the strand through forefinger, ringfinger, pinkie.
She could lace a basket, a boat
that could even carry water. *What to tip
the boatman?* I asked, trying to amuse her
with church and steeple turned to my empty palm.
Naptime, she'd lie there making shapes
above her, signing the air.

Later I saw the light touch in those twinned
fingertips had become her way
of holding still, keeping balance.
She had reached home before I did, finding
no mother at the bus stop, and entered
the silenced house for the first time alone.
Ancient, venerable, the whole place
waited, a relative with smells and creaks
she hesitated to greet. When I found her
she had made her way to the formal great room,
polite center of the hectic house where even

the clock's old thud gave back the heart
of simple waiting. Good guest, a shadow
on the rose Victorian settee, she sat,
her hands precise before her, an offering.

DEMETER

What woman can love that goddess?
Losing her own daughter,
she took a human child, believing
she could make him hers,
lay him in the gods' immortal fire
while the rightful mother slept.
Think of the mother's terror,
the rosy boy in the fireplace coals.
She yanked him away, burning
her hands and robe to smother flames—
took him back to our kind,
willing his eventual death.
Already she knew more than Demeter,
the homeless one who taught us
permanence has nothing to do with love.
As for the goddess, what would
the baby's eternal life have bought her?
Was her winter so easy
one child could replace another?

PERSEPHONE, ANSWERING

The girl in me died.
I watched her go under. In time
I turned back, answering the world
with my dead weight.
I entered the delirious air,
a spring I could make nothing of.

The question is
what is the end of grief?
I knew my mother then
for the first time: the bright self
withers, the soul
whitening like a stem that can't push its way
through rotted leaves, no balmy light
to fatten it into love

—if blooming is what we think is love.
Mother made herself into a bitter root,
living for a few days of flowering.
What art is that, always holding on?

FIST

The master talks about a life,
how it goes on building
dead coral, leaving something beautiful,
but this is not the way of children.
No, they take their lives elsewhere,
into thin air. The lost, the saved,
either way they disappear, their shapes
changing so intently that you come
back to them the way you revisit
a beloved shore, the mile of beach you'd known
like your own palm. This landmark
or that, shells coveted
for their rimmed blue—these pull you back,
but winters have passed. Did you only imagine

their brief, early bodies? Their fat hands
with the submerged knuckles, tender
indentations at the base of each finger,
each dot a marker for the bone
the weather of years would uncover.
Underneath that sweet fat, a future
composed itself, wintered and grew lean:
taught the hand to make itself a tool,
hold the toy, the spoon. And later, the knife,
the razor, the gun: instruments turned
against the self. A self grown by then
remote, rigid, unwilling to come back
to you, who nursed that body.

Remember the first months you tended it,
hour by hour; the years you checked it
sleeping, naptime and night time,

leaning over the breath's tide as if you
could trace it back to its start:
the rush of water, the rude air
invading the infant lungs, the gasp
which changed everything. Remember
that first time you unfurled
the tight fists, the initial strength
given the baby to save herself.

HISTORY

We called it "Life of Elvis," five sixth-grade girls
in sleep-over heaven. Mary Lane ruled us all,
claimed the part of Elvis, her man
since the cradle. She'd perfected his story
with the hips and knees, pantomiming
each song in her copy of his white-fringed
leather jacket, proof of how far he'd come
from the Sears jeans and Louisiana Hayride Show
right up the road in Bossier City.
When "It's All Right, Mama" hit the charts, Elvis
wriggled out of his contract and deeper
into our redneck hearts. We dedicated
our lives to his dog, his hunger
in a shotgun Mississippi shack, and Elvis' poor
mother, dead before the world knew who he was.
That true love moved us to his uplifted face
on his mother's favorite "Let Us Gather at the River"

and the night's business: her funeral.
Wrapped in a cotton sheet, I laid myself down
in the coffin built of couch cushions,
a camellia from the porch bush
bruising in my folded hands. Lights out
but the one forbidden candle, the weepers
took their turns until Elvis
buried her head in my bony chest.
Every Saturday night she taught me how
to hold the death pose, seducing
each breath, cutting it in half,
releasing it so slowly I almost passed out;
thrilled with Mary Lane and the passion
in the flower's clotted smell, the dying

we couldn't leave alone, the faith I'd cross
over to the other side. All I wanted
was to lie in that shallow grave.

WHAT DISAPPEARS

in Louisiana: start with a name,
birthright, stolen away
with my father's bus ride

to Texas and who-knows-where.
He took the Cherokee part of me,
left the Greek I traded

for a kind of English I'd later
slough off in shame. The color of skin
divided the town, kept me

from certain faces, the same ones
who left us peaches or purplehull peas
before dawn. Daylight swallowed them,

swallowed the cheap talk, childhood
with its hand-me-down dresses.
Years went their way, stripping

my brother's small esteem, that smile of his,
long before the night he vanished
from my mother's house. What disappears

is his body, sunk in the puzzle of the bayou.
I took myself out of that swamp,
took eighteen years, then came back

with love's intention. How can a place
be made for losing? Right out of my pocket,
the hair clip made of gold

from my good life, the leather purse
cradled on my lap. I won't turn my back
on my baby, my perfect blond boy

who's nine and wants to shake me off.
I hover while he's sleeping in my old bed.
I'm out on the porch, I'm watching.

RECONCILED

Spectators on the field, we saw
the horse gallop toward us,
froth whitening his face: no rider.
She darted out as if he'd called her.
Fighting past his weave and lunge,
she caught his neck as he reared, the reins
leaping past one hand, the other
scrambling for balance; her feet
in a dance with his digging hooves.
Somehow she grabbed and clutched—
when he felt the pull, he bucked
to break away, climbed the air
intending to drag her, but she tightened
with all her being
the black leather bounds in her fist.
No girl's strength could hold him,
nothing explains why he turned back to her,
stunned and waiting.

AN ELEGY

Even now she dreams of failure,
she the one who cannot rescue
the boy below the water
where he struggles, caught.
As she is caught in the minute
he has left, not breathing
but flailing down there, and she
the one who does not, cannot
see the hose coiled nearby in grass,
that hollow tube she could slice
with a pocket knife, passing it
to the one under water—the means
to air, to breath, to another life,
which of course is her own.
One expedient move, if only
she had the presence of mind
to see it waiting for her, but no,
her terror mirrors the terror
of the trapped boy; she does not
have the fortune of a sideways look,
nothing pulls her eye toward salvation,
and she wakes, wakes again,
as she will her whole life, her cold hand
reaching for the one she can never bring back.

She has taken this dream from a story
by Andre Dubus, who once sat with her,
lost at fifteen, locked
in her friend's death. But in his telling,
the narrator goes home and cuts
his garden hose in just the right lengths,
prepared from that point on.

This poem is for the one
who turned from darkness
and gave her the blessing of his gaze—Andre,
whose own great heart gave way.

OCULAR OCCLUSION

A certain kind of person
takes in what he sees, filling his eye
the way a breathing shellfish
takes sand. As one particle can settle
to make something lovely—lucent globe,
perfect whitening—
in him, something closes
over the thin lens that gives the eye
its sight. When he sleeps
everything the world has shown him
ceases its violation.
No longer is he the father
walking his three-year-old son,
who picks up a stick,
beating it on the beach path as they go,
until the one moment the father
glances at a bird passing, or
briefly inward, and then the scream
from nowhere, or everywhere, his head
filled with it: the sight of the stick
hanging from his fallen child's face.
No matter that by whatever grace
the child is fine, stitches
in the lucky spot, health and beauty
restored, and the father
spared. Only in sleep
does jeopardy recede as predictably
as the moon turns the sea in its bed.
No wonder when he wakes, the opening lid
rips apart the healing that began
in those safe hours. The longer the sleep,
the greater the pain

in the eye opening once again
to take it all in, receive the danger—
much as beach sand swells with the water
the tide drives in, as the mollusk
opens to the sifting flow,
as skin receives the knife.

SAVING HERSELF

Because my daughter loves the dog,
he is less dog than spirit.
He advises her dark center. The wolf
of intent and action, he answers
her low whistle. He's all hers,
tail and eye, one ear cocked,
as if he had been waiting all this time,
emissary of her own imagination,

born the same year of her friend's death.
That loss at fourteen remembers
the one at eight: childhood's black cat,
killed by hounds in the woods
where she had taken him to play.
Grief hastened her to a place
like the nowhere in fairy tales,
where a girl must take on trials

proving her worth to bring the loved one back.
But no live cat waited as the measure
of her goodness. No words she knew
could turn the key, save the cat
out of those red mouths: see now
whole again. No parent could undo
that bind, or see the path she'd take
to the friend who would be snatched away.

Lost in self-blame, she can't explain
the mystery of the dog, arriving
with his daily habits. She laughed
to see him lift one careful paw,
wet it with his tongue and rub it hard

along the side of his snout.
In the blessings of gaze and howl,
he showed her how to find

her way back. Who can say
what she sees now, the young woman
standing on the edge of the cultivated yard,
her animal at a distance
in the still-leafless trees? She watches
his body's white force
bounding in and out of sight, a flash
in the continuing black weave.

THE BOW

Protector of animals, director
of canine gymnastics, the parade of cats
persuaded to use the swing and slide;
believer in every creature's conversation
lent to her attentive ear, my daughter
is not content to simply be
the equestrienne. The elegant
dressage: sidestepping horse ballet,
the tight stadium round of jumps, breakneck
cross-country course over six-foot
gouges in the earth—none of these
matches her pride in her chestnut's
practiced bow. In the day-dark of the barn,
she lures him from his hay-flicked stall
where he faces the corner, planted and sullen,
feigning sleep until her lilt
says apple. His ear flickers, he shoves
his hind to the side, turns and shuffles out,
all seventeen hands of his bulk
intent on the thing in her hand. A thrill
ripples from his withers to his tail.
She lets him sniff just long enough
to tease, then lowers her arm
down his neck, the massive horse head
following as she reaches past his chest,
the rippling muscles in their neat divide
just over the heart; then further down,
where the spindly legs join his trunk.
When you think the horse can't possibly
bend his head to his belly, that the sheer
weight of his upper body
will collapse, undo every sinew and joint

in the trembling articulation,
he goes down on one knee,
one delicate motion, fetlock and hoof rising
back in a graceful arc. A courtier
who has learned every medieval charm, he
stretches his gorgeous nose, curves
his lips into her waiting palm.

THE GOODBYE

He's a child: he kisses the house.
It happens in an instant, a kiss
of affiliation, of letting go.
He's about to leave home,
the small changes in the room he's always had:
crib to bed, seasonal light
playing on the wall above his head,
the birch leaves waving across
his window. The house
is so familiar he may never know
exactly what he misses until one day
he wakes in a foreign room, seeing
the seamed angle of a roof,
silvered in the muted light,
or visiting an old house whose hint of must
takes him back with a stab.
Even then, experience will not be so much
recollected as it will have lived
all that time in the body,
setting up its severe household.
He'll be caught
outside himself, pausing
at the whole, its meaning laid before him
the way a child sets out all his things,
the many little engines lined up just so.

Wait, I have to go back for something,
he says, the sun about to fall
behind the century's trees, the old
place in its fullest gold.
He lays his whole body against the door
and presses the quick kiss, so quick

the parents in the car won't see.
What I know best about him
is how he stares off into the middle distance,
tongue thrust against the inside of his cheek
to let me know he does not want to talk,
the heart held at bay like some threatened
creature on the yard's edge,
the one that meets your eye
then retreats, finding its way
back into the woods.

UNDER MOOSE MOUNTAIN

1.

I spoke to the house: I am leaving you
I said. A house is not the world,
though it may serve as body. The house
is not flesh, though it held us
sometimes like a fist, sometimes
blowing into an ear with its silks
of light and air. Ghosts, we said at first,
catching the whisper as it flew past,
settling in the door frame, crooked
but holding everything up. The first year
I couldn't bear that hint of a voice
just over my shoulder. It sent me out
past the driveway into the woods,
the noisy layers of night I preferred
to fires in every room, the history
of breathing and dying an old house knows

—the way it knows children, and calls them,
answers the fact of their loneliness
with its own creaking as the child lies
watching in the night. Even I learned
to take that comfort, first a place
to house my fear, later a precious thing
I'd trade for my daughter's health.
That old sad note in her
still plays, echoing, lasting
like the row of maples dying on ledge
these last hundred years. What gets added
is her childhood, a little story
that came out right.

I walk through rooms, and this time
the dark is just an incidental thing,
a chipped bowl, a cradle in the corner,
part of what's been lived. Fifteen years
of stumbling over the uneven floors, random
nails appearing overnight on the scarred
pine boards, dependable as the groaning
farm truck at dawn, its empty bed
sounding in the loose windows. My footfall
rattles the teacups under glass,
every sound and slant of light tracing
back to the beginning, when that cabinet
was built into the wall. Where the sun

has always found it, sweeping over
the forked road, past the oak cradling
a fallen birch in the old V of its trunk,
past my thick work of summer flowers
in the bed I tamed from a slag pit,
lugging rocks away to dig
that front border deep enough
to sustain anything I planted.

2.

My daughter packs up the room I learned
to dread in the pitch-dark of its map.
Mild now in the afternoon,
it's stripped to the walls, the ceiling
painted once again. All winter,
moisture from the humidifier's drip
rose to sweat away the new white coat
from the layer of panicked scrawl, red
shoved into the black she fought

with a blade that scarred more than wood.
The revelation somehow

pleases her: a picked lock.
When you were sick: my smoothed voice
casual, turned away, not showing the girl
my grief for a place I want now to redeem,
not abandon. Naked, pale,
it stands empty, four walls and a floor
giving back the hollow of our voices.

Finished, she lets the silence
spin around her—nothing
as she pauses at the top of her stair,
a world surveyed one last time,
then clatters down. We quit her childhood,
we quit the house, an old relative
who holds the key to a few family years,
the real story living in that body
we know we won't see again. In this way

we all change places, she the mother
to the girl, and I—who will I be
when I finish all this sweeping and scrubbing,
part of me leaving,
walking out, locking the door?

FALL AT WELLFLEET BEACH

Scraps of foil, I think: someone's littered,
but the choppy glitter makes its way
down the beach. Closer, I see the little fish,
red-eyed, lying in twos or strangely head-to-tail.
Some heads are raised, gaping, as if to question

this new solid air where they've been chased
by a run of blues. Where I'm battling
the confined self. No children or surfers
in the crowd, just the bounty of fish and fishermen.
Victim and prey, the bluefish

struggle in the sand, changed
from their quicksilver light to dirty slabs.
They are swimming on ground, so intent on flight
they would pound all the way to hell
before they'd just lie still.

I walk past body after fighting body
until an old fisherman, set apart
for his lack of blues in the dug-out sand
behind him, asks if I want a fish.
He has one he's prying loose, freeing

with care the silver-rimmed mouth.
Still caught by their assigned grace, I refuse,
and he lifts that gleam of twisting metal by the tail
and wades into the breaking waves. The fish
flips back. He sticks his hand in

to hoist the frantic mass deeper. It aims
its body in a circling link, its compass fixed.

Lucky fish, I say, and the man grunts, *One a minute,*
meager exchange in this scene where everyone
takes something. One woman can't move fast enough,

stuffing smelts in a plastic grocery bag
as the raveling knot of gulls
strips their flesh up and down the beach.
Under the sun's flat blade, the crimped
ocean glints. I've had my fill of the feast,

of whatever fin slicing its way. I keep to
my own strict line on the buffer of plain sand
where the tide has come in, taking the carnage.
Poetry is a fine illusion, a moment. The sand
is cold enough. I don't let the water touch me.

HOUSE OF CLOCKS

Forget the colored leaves, simple time
commanding the trees. The trail's a test
around the hill—two miles,
twenty-four jumps, four minutes on a horse,
an alarm strapped to her wrist.
Blood type, allergies, year of birth
announce themselves on her black sleeve.

The hillside is a wayward house,
each room a hazard of jumps
set out like furniture to trip her up.
Too early in the start box, the horse
backs and shies, mad for the first forgiving
rails on the beaten path. Her chiming voice
guides him through the maze,

in and out of tunneled light, answering
the question of each jump—until the trick
of a sharp left blinded by the hill,
a circle she can't break or he will fail
the dark door among the trees.
Her safety lies in two extremes:
outriding the chaos in her head

and minding the metronome of hoofbeats,
solid time I can hear with my palm
pressed to the ground. In late afternoon's
auburn light, the burnish of her braided hair
goes red, red as her chestnut, and they blur past
in a season standing still—through the gate
and old bridge over the tired pond

to the stairs of the bank that sends them
flying into nothing, a kind of heaven
this horse never fears. She knows enough
to stay back, throwing her faith
to his leap, racing the clock.
He'll do the giant table, stone walls,
but he will falter at the water's flicker,

and the coffin looms ahead, six feet
carved out of the field. Where I've chosen
to wait, where the sporadic file and grate
of one cricket is all I hear.
It's autumn, when we close the doors,
and nothing answers the silence
but that mechanical song.

GATEKEEPER

It's a relief when it goes:
the thrall of leaves, a demiurge
in the treetops, after the bliss
of waiting gold. Before the dead season,
we recognize the dead. The dog searches,
nose down, trailing something rank
to roll in and wear as the sign of who he is
under the thumb of Saturn—the god
who ate all his children but the ones of air.
What's left, I wonder
in November, but the shimmering ground, still
lit with leaves, their feast-like colors
underfoot. On the path to the river
I see the shape that lends the land
its rise and fall. Clarity informs me
like the distant-eyed
gaze of the chipmunk left at my door,
the hour it took to die, the quiver in him
driven by a disbelieving heart, his back legs
rowing and rowing, nothing in him so great
as the need to get up, get to the other side.

THE BETRAYAL

Before the dog came, I never knew
about the woods in snow, knee-high; never fell
on the pathless maze that led me in.
Off his leash, he remembered who he'd been—
a raving thing, roaming, and he threw
his whole body in a run, a forward motion
that sank him, rocked him, the long thrust
upward from his hind. He put his snout
down deep in the layered cold
and tunneled, longing after
some hidden thing he knew was there
if only he could dig it out. Some dying smell
guided him to frenzy, and he turned,
pretending not to know me: he was beast, and I
owned the stick, which to him became bone,
the marrow he needed to survive, and so he leapt
in circles around me, pulling closer, madder,
his growls deepening, his eyes going flat
and foreign. I put aside my fear,
put the stick between us and held on
with everything I had. I lowered my head
and fought, laying my flesh on his.
I smelled the hot breath, felt the cold black
tip of his nose; I allowed the two bared fangs
to touch my lower lip: the moment
when he could have had me.
But in that pause, he pulled away
with a long canine sigh, lifted his face
all the way up to the great slow rocking
in the tops of the pines, the sifting ash-like
snow that followed downward like a whisper.
He froze, caught; his open mouth quivered.

Long ago, he raged for meat, knew the damned
before they knew themselves. He stood
with the gods and did their bidding.
Love had nothing to do with it.

DEMETER THE PILGRIM

Love, she thought, would bring her back,
so she took the guise of crone,
black robes, gaunt face reflecting
the agony that had brought her
to the sisters at the well. She was searching,
crying, reduced from goddess
to one with an arm outstretched.
Even human pity would do, a human child.
For aren't all babies alike
in their physical, grasping selves,
their unmediated need?

A hurricane, a famine.
Who could deny the weather, the iron ocean
rocking, the fear they all would break
in the end. An old woman—
who wouldn't take her in?

She made herself useful, tending
the hearth, the infant who had learned
to babble and reach. When she took him
in her arms, head against her breast,
all the green world washed over her,
smell and touch returned to the source.

You know the story. We've passed it down,
a token in the gray landscape, a winter
you make your own. Once again,
it's not so much the actual moment
the girl is snatched away, but the watching,
time waiting with its noose,
all your terror balanced there.

And the future
slides out like the fog offshore,
its own continent
floating between the sea and sky.

FIGURE OF FORMAL LOSS: PEARL

—for Faith Knapp

No longer someone's mother,
she's still a woman, doing the usual chores.
Now she's bending over melons, a fragrant
pile in the grocery store, a laden basket.
And there it is: gold, swollen to its ultimate
paleness, a great globe, the skin so thinned
and stretched against the heavy flesh
she can almost see through it. The blossom end
with its slight bulge, almost the soft spot
on a baby's head—she can imagine a pulse
in the fruit. Bending there, caught in the luxury
of choosing among so many lovelinesses, she
doesn't know her own rapt face. She's moved back
to the sea, transported there,
reminded in the mind's way
of the outline barely discernible in the low fog's
nothingness, wet gray cast over the morning.
She's walking through it again, drifting forward,
following the white line the water makes,
its thread of continuity that keeps her
moving. How far can she walk this way, how long
can stasis define the available heavens,
the miles of beach she thought she knew?
She thinks of the sun out there, that gold ball
suspended over the eastern sea, and then her own
dull settling of densities, the cold veil she wears—
how can any light ever break through?

Now with melons, in the middle of an ordinary morning,
this happens: the sea and its obscure sun

brought back whole, and she is swallowing hard
to keep hold of a moment that has somehow
moved her beyond acceptance,
passing through all suffering to the core.
Not willed or understood, not some mood
traversing the surfaces of self, a temporary
easing of the burden. No, it's as if
her dead child has curled into some accommodating
spirit, an abiding that settles into its own place.
The child curled on her side, sleeping
as children sleep, bound up like a fist, turned inward
as if to protect. A grain, a speck, so insistent
that the self forms its layers around it
one thickness at a time, at first gray, the sullen
lubricant accruing, and as it grows, hardening,
taking on a luster, a lightening of the mineral.
Until, degree by degree, every sorrow goes pure,
brightening its coat, still forming itself
over the kernel of the child who is not
so much the child she made inside her, but her own
particle of self. The child as a figure of formal loss,
and over it, the luminous shell of her own being:
a shining that passes for who she is.

LIVING HERE

In the absence of ocean, I have the field
and I walk there with the dogs
on a chain. One who won't shut up,
the other large and grave
with his patient look—we all survey
gray sky, gray woods, absence
turning the season. A scrimshaw of ice
is water's only possibility.
The field is married to silence, a cloud
lying across it, and when it lifts
no horizon takes my eye. No glory of night
falling at sea, light's limitless plane.
In the field, containment
is everything, locked as it is
by evergreen shade. The ground
darkens to a threat.
Why not accept the bounds,
love the confined self?
In the world of appearances, teach me
to believe in the unseen.
I watch where I put my foot—no sound
in this universe but that reassuring thud.

BIOGRAPHICAL NOTE

Cleopatra Mathis was born and raised in Ruston,
Louisiana. Since 1982 she has lived with her family in
Hanover, New Hampshire, where she is Professor of
English and Creative Writing at Dartmouth College.

OTHER BOOKS BY CLEOPATRA MATHIS PUBLISHED BY
THE SHEEP MEADOW PRESS:
Guardian (1995)
The Center for Cold Water (1989)
The Bottom Land (1983)
Aerial View of Louisiana (1979)